# Harriet and Walt

Original Story by Nancy Carlson

Script and Lyrics by Jennifer Kirkeby
Music by Shirley Mier

Single copies of plays are sold for reading purposes only. The copying or duplicating of a play, or any part of play, by hand or by any other process, is an infringement of the copyright. Such infringement will be vigorously prosecuted.

**Baker's Plays**
**7611 Sunset Blvd.**
**Los Angeles, CA 90042**
**BAKERSPLAYS.COM**

**NOTICE**

This book is offered for sale at the price quoted only on the understanding that, if any additional copies of the whole or any part are necessary for its production, such additional copies will be purchased. The attention of all purchasers is directed to the following: this work is fully protected under the copyright laws of the United States of America, the British Commonwealth, including Canada, and all other countries of the Copyright Union. Violations of the Copyright Law are punishable by fine or imprisonment, or both. The copying or duplication of this work or any part of this work, by hand or by any process, is an infringement of the copyright and will be vigorously prosecuted.

This play may not be produced by amateurs or professionals for public or private performance without first submitting application for performing rights. Licensing fees are due on all performances whether for charity or gain, or whether admission is charged or not. Since performance of this play without the payment of the royalty fee renders anybody participating liable to severe penalties imposed by the law, anybody acting in this play should be sure, before doing so, that the royalty fee has been paid. Professional rights, reading rights, radio broadcasting, television and all mechanical rights, etc. are strictly reserved. Application for performing rights should be made directly to BAKER'S PLAYS.

No one shall commit or authorize any act or omission by which the copyright of, or the right to copyright, this play may be impaired. No one shall make any changes in this play for the purpose of production.

Publication of this pl0ay does not imply availability for performance. Both amateurs and professionals considering a production are strongly advised in their own interest to apply to Baker's Plays for written permission before starting rehearsals, advertising, or booking a theatre.

Whenever the play is produced, the author's name must be carried in all publicity, advertising and programs. Also, the following notice must appear on all printed programs, "Produced by special arrangement with Baker's Plays."

Licensing fees for HARRIET AND WALT are based on a per performance rate and payable one week in advance of the production.

Please consult the Baker's Plays website at www.bakersplays.com or our current print catalogue for up to date licensing fee information.

Book and Lyrics Copyright © 2010 by Jennifer Kirkeby
Made in U.S.A.
All rights reserved.
Illustrations © 1992 by Nancy Carlson, all rights reserved

HARRIET AND WALT
ISBN 978-0-87440-234-6
# 2029-B

No one shall commit or authorize any act or omission by which the copyright of, or the right to copyright, this play may be impaired.

No one shall make any changes in this play for the purpose of production.

Publication of this play does not imply availability for performance. Both amateurs and professionals considering a production are strongly advised in their own interests to apply to Samuel French, Inc., for written permission before starting rehearsals, advertising, or booking a theatre.

No part of this book may be reproduced, stored in a retrieval system, or transmitted in any form, by any means, now known or yet to be invented, including mechanical, electronic, photocopying, recording, videotaping, or otherwise, without the prior written permission of the publisher.

## RENTAL MATERIALS

An orchestration consisting of a Piano/Vocal Score and Vocal Chorus Book will be loaned two months prior to the production ONLY on the receipt of the Licensing Fee quoted for all performances, the rental fee and a refundable deposit.

Please contact Baker's Plays for perusal of the musis materials as well as a performance license application.

## IMPORTANT BILLING AND CREDIT REQUIREMENTS

All producers of *HARRIET AND WALT* must give credit to the Author of the Play in all programs distributed in connection with performances of the Play, and in all instances in which the title of the Play appears for the purposes of advertising, publicizing or otherwise exploiting the Play and/or a production. The name of the Author *must* appear on a separate line on which no other name appears, immediately following the title and *must* appear in size of type not less than fifty percent of the size of the title type.

In addition the following credit *must* be given in all programs and publicity information distributed in association with this piece except those licensed by Stages Theatre Company, Hopkins, Minnesota:

**Original commission by Stages Theatre Company,
Hopkins, Minnesota**

**Adapted from the book by Nancy Carlson**

***HARRIET AND WALT*** was commissioned and first produced by Stages Theatre Company; artistic director, Sandy Boren-Barrett. It premiered January 19, 2007, at Stages Theatre Company in Hopkins, Minnesota, with the following cast and production team:

| | |
|---|---|
| **LOUANNE** | Nikki Akingbasote |
| **HARRIET** | Megan Collins |
| **AUNT SUSAN** | Celia Forrest |
| **SYDNEY** | Emilee Hassanzadeh |
| **ARNIE** | Zachary Mahler |
| **BALLERINA & KELLY** | Dori Meifert |
| **OSWALDO** | Anders Nerheim |
| **JENNY & YOUNG NANCY** | Caila Paquin |
| **WALT** | Noah Paquin |
| **KATHERINE & YOUNG SUSAN** | Scout Peterson |
| **NANCY** | Lizzie Rainville |
| **TINA** | Asia Thornton |
| **GEORGE** | Jesse Vallera |

| | |
|---|---|
| Director | Marilee Mahler |
| Production Manager | Melanie Salmon-Peterson |
| Stage Manager | Angie Hardy |
| Music Director | Melissa Brunkan |
| Choreographer | Angela Mannella |
| Set Designer | Kate Sutton-Johnson |
| Props Designer | Jim Hibbeler |
| Costume/Make-up Designer | Lisa LeGrand |
| Lighting Designer | Joe Stanley |
| Sound Board Operator | Madi Brunkan |
| Light Board Operators | Caroline Casey & Christine Silikowski |
| Original Illustrations | Nancy Carlson |

## CHARACTERS

(2 adults or older teens, 11 children)

**HARRIET** (Dog, F) – Older sister of Walt. Loves winter.
**NANCY** (Dog, F) – Harriet's Mom, Adult or older teen.
**SUSAN** (Dog, F) – Harriet's eccentric and fun-loving Aunt, Adult or older teen.
**WALT** (Dog, M) – Harriet's little brother. He loves to rhyme.

## HARRIET'S FRIENDS

**LOUANNE** (Pig, F) – Harriet's best friend. Happy-go-lucky.
**GEORGE** (Rabbit, M) – Competitive.
**SYDNEY** (Chihuahua, F) – Very smart.
**OSWALDO** (Dog, M) – Reflective.
**ARNIE** (Cat, M) – Good-natured and kind.
**TINA** (Beaver, F) – Cheerful.
**KELLY** (Rabbit, F) & **BALLERINA**
**KATHERINE & YOUNG SUSAN** (Dog, F)
**JENNY & YOUNG NANCY** (Dog, F)

## SCENES

Scene #1: Harriet's House (Kitchen) & Outside
Scene #2: Harriet's House
Scene #3: Harriet's House & Outside
Scene #4: Outside of Harriet's House
Scene #5: Harriet's House
Scene #6: The Winter Carnival
Scene #7: The Winter Carnival Dance

## SONGS

1. Yippee! (**KIDS**) (Scene 1)
2. Boys (**HARRIET** & **LOUANNE**) (Scene 2)
3. Snow Globe Lullaby (**NANCY**) (Scene 2)
4. Don't Forget Walt (**KIDS**) (Scene 3)
5. The Snowman Race (**KIDS**) (Scene 4)
6. What Would I Do Without You? (**NANCY** & **SUSAN**) (Sc. 5)
7. The Snowman Race Reprise (**KIDS**) (Scene 6)
8. Winter Carnival Dance (**ALL**) (Scene 7)

*This play is dedicated to Noah Paquin*

## Scene One

*(After pre-show music, lights go down and a special comes up on* **HARRIET** *in her bedroom. She is holding a Snow Globe that she winds up. Winding sound effects, then* ***SONG No. 1: YIPPEE!*** *intro (music box underscore) begins.* **HARRIET** *shakes her Snow Globe, puts it down and exits. Lights go down except on the Snow Globe. Lights shift from* **HARRIET***'s Snow Globe to a large "Snow Globe" onstage. (Please see Set Design info in back of script.) It begins to snow. A* **BALLERINA** *begins to dance inside the Snow Globe. Music Box underscore ends; music changes and lights shift to* **HARRIET** *in her kitchen. She looks outside and sees her friends playing in the snow.)*

**HARRIET.** Yippee! It's snowing! And all of my friends are playing! Can I *please* go outside and play with them, Mom? *Please?*

**NANCY.** After you help put away the breakfast, Harriet.

**HARRIET.** But by then it might be done snowing! Oh *please?*

**NANCY.** After the dishes are done, dear. Then you may go out.

*(Lights up onstage.* ***YIPPEE!*** *music is playing. The stage is a winter wonderland.* **ARNIE, GEORGE, OSWALDO, LOUANNE, TINA & SYDNEY** *are throwing snowballs, building snowmen, making snow angels, laughing, etc.* **HARRIET** *and* **WALT** *are inside their house finishing their breakfast with* **NANCY**, *their mom. The* **KIDS** *sing :)*

***SONG No. 1: YIPPEE!***

**KIDS.**
YIPPEE! IT'S SNOWING! I'VE WAITED ALL YEAR LONG!
YIPPEE! IT'S WINTER! SO LET'S ALL SING THIS SONG!

WE'LL BE SLEDDING DOWN BIG HILLS OF WHITE AND
  LAUGHING AS WE GO.
THERE ISN'T ANYTHING SO FINE AS FIELDS AND FIELDS OF
  SNOW!
YIPPEE! IT'S SNOWING! I'VE WAITED ALL YEAR LONG!
YIPPEE! IT'S WINTER! SO LET'S ALL SING THIS SONG!
SKATING, SKIING, SNOWBALLS TOO, WE'LL WATCH THEM
  SOAR AND FLY!
WE'LL BUILD A GIANT SNOWMAN AND HE WILL TOUCH
  THE SKY!
AND HE WILL TOUCH THE SKY!

*(Underscoring plays throughout the following dialogue.* **HARRIET** *quickly begins to put the dishes away and tries to hurry* **WALT** *along with his eating.)*

**HARRIET.** Hurry up Walt so I can put away your plate.

**WALT.** Plate…great!

**NANCY.** Very good, Walt! *(to* **HARRIET***)* Walt's been learning how to rhyme!

**HARRIET.** If only he could actually help clean up.

**NANCY.** He will when he's a little older. *(watches* **HARRIET***)* Slow down young lady before you break a dish.

**WALT.** Dish…fish!

**NANCY.** Good rhyming, Walt! Now finish eating so Harriet can see her friends.

**HARRIET.** *(to* **WALT***)* Eat!

**WALT.** Eat…feet!

**HARRIET.** Mom! He's never going to be done! Can't I just go now, *please!*

**NANCY.** In a minute, Harriet.

**HARRIET.** Aughhh!

**SOLOS/GROUPS.**
LET'S ALL BUILD A SNOWMAN!
I JUST WANT TO SKATE,
WE JUST GOT A BRAND NEW SLED,
ALL OF IT SOUNDS SO GREAT.
WATCH OUT FOR THAT SNOWBALL!

IT'S FLYING THROUGH THE AIR.
WINTER IS OUR FAV'RITE TIME (WINTER IS OUR FAV'RITE TIME),
WE HAVEN'T GOT A CARE (WE HAVEN'T GOT A CARE!)

**ALL.**
YIPPEE! IT'S SNOWING! I'VE WAITED ALL YEAR LONG!
YIPPEE! IT'S WINTER! SO LET'S ALL SING THIS SONG!
WE'LL BE SLEDDING DOWN BIG HILLS OF WHITE AND LAUGHING AS WE GO.
THERE ISN'T ANYTHING SO FINE AS FIELDS AND FIELDS OF SNOW!

(*Underscoring continues as* **HARRIET** *runs to the window and waves to her friends. They wave back and call to her to come outside.*)

**KIDS.** (*staggered*) Hi Harriet! Come outside! It's snowing! Let's build a fort! Hurry up, Harriet! (*etc.*)

**HARRIET.** I'll be out soon! Mom! Everything's put away! My friends *need* me! May I please go outside now?

**NANCY.** (*as she wipes off* **WALT**'s *face and hands.*) Yes, Harriet, you may go outside now.

**HARRIET.** Hurray!

(*She rushes to put her coat on.*)

**NANCY.** Oh, Harriet?

**HARRIET.** Yes, mom?

**NANCY.** Don't forget Walt.

**HARRIET.** *What?* Do I *have* to take him?

(**WALT** *begins clapping and smiling broadly. He runs over to* **HARRIET** *and hugs her. He continues hugging her during the following lines:*)

**NANCY.** Honey, it will be good for both of you. Fresh air, exercise…why, when I was your age we would go outside all day long. It will be fun! Look how much he loves you. I'll help him get dressed while you put your coat on.

**HARRIET.** Oh fine. (**WALT** *is still hugging* **HARRIET** *as she tries to move away.*) Let go of me, Walt!

NANCY. Come here, Walt. Let's put your coat on.

(WALT *runs to* NANCY *who begins to bundle him up.* HARRIET *quickly puts on her coat, hat and gloves.*)

WALT. Coat...goat!

NANCY. *(to* WALT*)* Very good, honey! Harriet, do you have a word that Walt can rhyme?

HARRIET. Sure. Pain.

NANCY. Harriet...

WALT. Pain...rain!

HARRIET. Late!

WALT. Late...great!

HARRIET. I'm leaving!

WALT. Leaving...

HARRIET. COME ON, WALT!!!

*(She takes his hand and they walk outside.)*

KIDS. *(staggered)* Hi Harriet! Hey Walt! Glad you're here! *(etc.)*

HARRIET. Hi everyone!

TINA. We thought that you'd never get here!

HARRIET. Neither did I.

OSWALDO. Hi Walt! How's it going little guy?

WALT. Good...mud!

OSWALDO. Good mud? What's he talking about, Harriet?

HARRIET. He's learning to rhyme.

OSWALDO. Are you sure?

ARNIE. We haven't started the Snowman Race yet.

SYDNEY. According to my calculations, it's a superb day for compacting snow.

GEORGE. Is that a good thing?

SYDNEY. Of course! One must compact in order for one to achieve the best snowman.

GEORGE. I knew that.

LOUANNE. Boy, Sydney sure is smart!

HARRIET. She sure is! Louanne, did you ask if you can spend the night?

**LOUANNE.** Yes, and I can.

**HARRIET.** Great!

**TINA.** Aren't you excited about the Winter Carnival?

**HARRIET.** We sure are!

**LOUANNE.** I can't wait!

**HARRIET.** Yippee! I'm so excited to be outside! I've waited a whole year for this!

**SOLOS/GROUPS.**
>WATCH ME MAKE A SNOW ANGEL,
>THEN WE'RE GOING TO SKI!

**ARNIE.**
>I GOT BUNDLED UP SO TIGHT,
>THAT I CAN'T EVEN SEE!

**ALL.**
>ALL THE WORLD LOOKS MAGICAL,
>IT'S BEAUTIFUL AND WHITE,
>IF OUR PARENTS WOULD LET US,
>WE'D STAY OUT HERE ALL NIGHT!
>
>YIPPEE! IT'S SNOWING! I'VE WAITED ALL YEAR LONG!
>YIPPEE! IT'S WINTER! SO LET'S ALL SING THIS SONG!
>SKATING, SKIING, SNOWBALLS TOO, WE'LL WATCH THEM SOAR AND FLY!
>WE'LL BUILD A GIANT SNOWMAN AND HE WILL TOUCH THE SKY!
>AND HE WILL TOUCH THE SKY!
>YIPPEE!

**SYDNEY.** O.K. everybody! It's time to practice for the Snowman Race!

**GEORGE.** Ready to make the snowman, Harriet?

**HARRIET.** I sure am!

*(WALT follows HARRIET.)*

**GEORGE.** Uh, Harriet?

**HARRIET.** Yes, George?

**GEORGE.** Does Walt have to tag along?

**HARRIET.** He won't get in the way. I just need to watch him today.

**GEORGE.** Oh. Too bad.

**WALT.** Bad...sad.

**HARRIET.** Good job, Walt!

**GEORGE.** At least that time it rhymed.

**TINA.** Come on everybody!

(**ARNIE** *throws a snowball at* **TINA.**)

**TINA.** Hey!

(**ARNIE** *laughs.* **TINA** *throws a snowball back at* **ARNIE.**)

**ARNIE.** Snowball fight!

(**KIDS** *laugh and begin to throw snowballs at each other.*)

**SYDNEY.** FOCUS PLEASE!

**GEORGE.** Arnie started it!

**ARNIE.** Tattle tale.

**KIDS.** Shhh!

(**KIDS** *stop throwing snowballs and get ready to practice.*)

**OSWALDO.** I hope that we win the Snowman Race this year!

**TINA.** Me too. But Sydney said that we're behind last year's record by 3 seconds.

**SYDNEY.** *(looks at her stopwatch)* That's true. By my calculations, if we minimize the compacting of the snow when we create the large pieces, we should be able to take off 2 seconds. Are you ready?

**KIDS.** Ready!

**SYDNEY.** On your mark. (**KIDS** *get into positions.*) Get set. Go!

*(No. 1A SNOWMAN RACE Underscore plays:)*

(**KIDS** *begin a carefully choreographed "building a snowman" race. They make the base, body, head, eyes, ears, nose and mouth. (See Snowman construction info in the back of script.)* **KIDS** *are yelling and encouraging each other to "do a good job, but go faster!"* **HARRIET** *is about to put the head on.* **WALT** *tries to "help" but ends up knocking down the snowman.*)

**HARRIET.** Walt, no! *(to her friends)* I'm sorry. Walt was just trying to help.

**GEORGE.** Well, he sure didn't. Walt is a pest, Harriet.

(**WALT** *looks sad. He picks up the head of the snowman and hands it to* **HARRIET**.)

**WALT.** Head…dead.

(**KIDS** *laugh except for* **GEORGE**.)

**LOUANNE.** Good rhyming!

**TINA.** It's O.K., Walt!

**OSWALDO.** It could have happened to any of us!

**GEORGE.** Not me.

**ARNIE.** He didn't mean to knock it down.

**OSWALDO.** Actually, this reminds me of the time that I was about to make a touchdown. I was running as fast as I could, everyone was yelling with excitement, the wind was rushing by me and all of a sudden…

(**OSWALDO** *gets quiet. Everyone is waiting for him to finish.*)

**KIDS.** Yeah…?

**GEORGE.** Well, what happened, Oswaldo?

**OSWALDO.** I'd rather not talk about it.

(**KIDS** *look at each other and shrug.*)

**LOUANNE.** Come on everybody! We'll just start over!

**SYDNEY.** Uh, Harriet?

**HARRIET.** Yes, Sydney?

**SYDNEY.** Could Walt just sit and watch? That way I can get a true reading of the time.

**GEORGE.** Great idea!

**HARRIET.** Oh, sure.

(**HARRIET** *takes* **WALT**'s *hand and guides him away from the snowman.*)

Walt, you need to sit over here while we make the snowman, O.K.?

**WALT.** Sit………knit.

**HARRIET.** Good job, Walt! Here, you can make your own snowman, all right?

**HARRIET.** *(gives him a few snowballs to play with)* I'll come help you when I'm done with my friends! Won't that be fun?

**WALT.** Fun…run!

**HARRIET.** Right. Now you stay here, and I'll be right back!

*(She rushes over to her friends.)*

Ready!

**SYDNEY.** On your mark! Get set! Go!

*(No. 1B SNOWMAN RACE Underscore plays.)*

*(The **KIDS** make the snowman as before. It is a success.)*

**KIDS.** Hurray! We did it! Way to go! *(etc.)*

**TINA.** What was our time, Sydney?

**SYDNEY.** We shaved off 2.836 seconds. Getting better!

**HARRIET.** Do you think the eyes are big enough?

*(**KIDS** inspect snowman.)*

**LOUANNE.** Harriet has a point. They do seem a little small.

**ARNIE.** You know what they say; the eyes are the windows to your soul.

*(**KIDS** look into each other's eyes then shrug.)*

**GEORGE.** Who cares about that? It's about the speed, not how the face looks.

**SYDNEY.** I'm sure that the judges will take everything into consideration, George. The proportions should be accurate.

**OSWALDO.** We can just use something bigger for the eyes.

**TINA.** Here, I have something!

*(**TINA** finds two objects for larger eyes. She hands them to **ARNIE**.)*

Try these.

*(**WALT** has become bored. He walks over to see what the **KIDS** are doing. No one notices him.)*

**ARNIE.** Thanks, Tina.

(**ARNIE** *carefully takes off the old eyes and begins to put on the new ones. As he replaces the second eye,* **WALT** *gets excited, and begins yelling and clapping his hands.*)

**WALT.** *(clapping his hands.)* Hurray! Eyes...pies!

**ARNIE.** *(startled)* Aughhh!

(**ARNIE** *accidentally knocks over the head of the snowman. He laughs.*)

You scared me little fella!

**HARRIET.** Not again! Walt! What did I tell you?

(**WALT** *looks very sad.*)

**GEORGE.** We are never going to win at this rate!

**LOUANNE.** *(Crosses to* **WALT** *and gives him a hug.)* Don't blame Walt. He's just excited.

**OSWALDO.** I suppose that's true. We should be able to work with distractions. Once when I was the goalie in the first grade, the other team was coming at me and I was ready to block except all of a sudden this huge bird started squaking and I... *(He stops.)*

**ARNIE.** And...?

**TINA.** You what, Oswaldo?

**KIDS.** *(staggered)* Yeah, what happened? Tell us Oswaldo. We want to know! *(etc.)*

**OSWALDO.** *(beat)* Some things are better left unsaid.

**ARNIE.** *(pats him on the shoulder)* It's O.K. Oswaldo. Winning isn't everything.

**OSWALDO.** Thanks, Arnie.

**GEORGE.** OH FOR CRYING OUT LOUD! CAN WE GET TO WORK OR WHAT?

**SYDNEY.** Well, what do we think, team? Bigger eyes?

**ARNIE.** I liked the bigger eyes. At least what I saw of them.

**SYDNEY.** O.K. then. Bigger eyes it is. As long as it doesn't affect our speed.

**NANCY.** *(calls outside)* Harriet! Walt! Time to come in now!

**HARRIET.** I'll see you tonight Louanne!

**LOUANNE.** See you then!

**SYDNEY.** I'll go and make some calculations to help us with our speed factoring in distractions as well as the eye weight factor.

(**SYDNEY** *exits.*)

**ALL KIDS.** (*except* **GEORGE, HARRIET & WALT**) (*staggered*) Bye! See you! Thanks, Sydney! (*etc.*)

(**KIDS** *exit.*)

**GEORGE.** Uh, Harriet?

**HARRIET.** Yes, George?

(**WALT** *is between them watching each one when they speak.*)

**GEORGE.** Can I call you later?

**HARRIET.** Sure!

**GEORGE.** O.K. So, I'll call you.

**HARRIET.** O.K.! (*pause*)

**GEORGE.** (*beat*) So…bye!

(*He runs off.*)

**HARRIET.** (*happily*) Bye!

(**HARRIET** *takes* **WALT** *by the hands and leads him home.*)

(***No. 1C YIPPEE! Scene Shift*** *music plays.*)

## Scene Two

*(Later that night.* **HARRIET & LOUANNE** *are in* **HARRIET***'s room. They are eating popcorn.)*

**HARRIET.** So I said: "Oh, I just love to dance. I've been taking ballet since I was 5, but I enjoy all kinds of dancing: tap, jazz, lyrical, even ballroom – although I don't know how to do it – I still like it because it's so graceful and I just feel like it's a wonderful expression of ourselves and how we feel about life and the world," and then George asked me to the dance at the Winter Carnival!

**LOUANNE.** *(giggling)* You really said all that?

**HARRIET.** Yes. I was a little nervous, I guess. Now you have to tell me!

**LOUANNE.** Well, I said: "Arnie, do you want to go to the Winter Carnival Dance with me?" And he said: "O.K."

**HARRIET.** *(beat)* That's it?

**LOUANNE.** Pretty much. Oh, he did ask me something.

**HARRIET.** *(excited)* What? *What?*

**LOUANNE.** He asked for the ketchup.

**HARRIET.** The ketchup?

**LOUANNE.** Yeah. We were at lunch.

**HARRIET.** Oh. *(beat)* What are you going to wear?

**LOUANNE.** I haven't really thought about it. Probably a dress.

**HARRIET.** Hmmm. I think you could use some fashion tips. I'd be glad to help.

**LOUANNE.** O.K.

**HARRIET.** What color is the dress you'll be wearing?

**LOUANNE.** Pink. No, red. Maybe blue. I haven't decided.

**HARRIET.** This is more serious than I thought. You want to make an impression don't you?

**LOUANNE.** I guess…

**HARRIET.** You want to look nice for Arnie, don't you?

**LOUANNE.** I suppose...

**HARRIET.** Here. Let me show you a dress that you'll look wonderful in!

**LOUANNE.** Right now?

**HARRIET.** Sure! No time like the present!

**LOUANNE.** Well, O.K.

(**LOUANNE** *begins to giggle.*)

***SONG No. 2: BOYS (intro)***

**HARRIET.** (*gets different dresses, accessories, etc. She gives* **LOUANNE** *a dress.* **LOUANNE** *holds it up to herself as she looks in the "mirror."*) What's so funny?

(**LOUANNE** *continues to giggle.*)

**HARRIET.** Louanne! Tell me! Is it this dress?

**LOUANNE.** No, no! Nothing like that. It's just that, well... I'm nervous about the dance.

**HARRIET.** Is that all?

(**HARRIET** *begins to giggle.*)

**LOUANNE.** What are *you* giggling about?

**HARRIET.** Oh, nothing.

(*She continues to giggle.*)

**LOUANNE.** Come on! I told you why *I* was laughing!

**HARRIET.** Well, I was just thinking that...that... *George is cute!*

(*They both scream with laughter.*)

**LOUANNE.** And I was just thinking that...oh, I can't say it!

**HARRIET.** Say it, Louanne!

**LOUANNE.** Oh, all right! *Arnie is cute too!*

(*They both giggle and laugh. As they sing the following song, they use the various clothes to dress up in – hats, boas, jewelry, etc.* **LOUANNE** *ends up with a dress on.*)

(**HARRIET** *and* **LOUANNE** *sing:*)

**BOTH.**
> BOYS, BOYS, THEY MAKE US GIGGLE! (TEE-HEE!)
> BOYS, BOYS, THEY MAKE US SMI-EE-I-EE-ILE.
> BOYS, BOYS, THEY KEEP US BUSY,
> AND VERY VERSATILE!

**LOUANNE.** *(spoken)*
> ARNIE IS KIND, SENSITIVE AND BRIGHT.
> HE ALWAYS THINKS OF OTHERS AND DOES WHAT IS RIGHT.
> HE'S HONEST, HE LISTENS AND HE TRIES TO BE OBJECTIVE,
> THE OTHER THING I LIKE IS THAT HE'S GOT A CAT'S PERSPECTIVE!

**HARRIET.** *(spoken)*
> GEORGE IS ENERGETIC, HE CAN GET THINGS DONE.
> WHEN HE HAS TO GO SOMEWHERE, HE ALWAYS RUNS.
> IT'S NEVER HARD TO FIND HIM, EVEN IN A CROWD,
> YOU'LL ALWAYS HEAR HIS VOICE BECAUSE IT'S JUST SO LOUD!

**BOTH.**
> BOYS, BOYS, THEY MAKE US GIGGLE!

**HARRIET.** *(spoken)*
> I LIKE GEORGE, HE IS A BUNNY, I HOPE HE WILL BE MY HONEY!

**BOTH.**
> BOYS, BOYS, THEY MAKE US SMILE!

**LOUANNE.**
> ARNIE IS A DARLING KITTY, WHEN I'M WITH HIM I FEEL GIDDY!

**BOTH.**
> BOYS, BOYS, THEY KEEP US BUSY,
> AND VERY VERSATILE!

**HARRIET.**
> WHEN I SEE GEORGE HOPPING 'ROUND THE PLACE,
> HE PUTS A SMILE RIGHT ON MY FACE!

**LOUANNE.**
> IT'S SO FINE TO BE A SWINE,
> WON'T YOU BE MY VALENTINE?

**BOTH**. *(spoken)*
> OOH, ARNIE, YOU'RE SO FINE, WON'T YOU BE MY VALENTINE!

**BOTH**.
> BOYS, BOYS, THEY MAKE US GIGGLE! (TEE HEE!)
> BOYS, BOYS, THEY MAKE US SMI-EE-I-EE-ILE!
> BOYS, BOYS, THEY KEEP US BUSY,
> AND VERY VERSATILE!
>
> (**GIRLS** *giggle and then recover.*)
>
> AND VERY VERSATILE!
>
> (**WALT** *begins knocking loudly on* **HARRIET***'s door.*)

**HARRIET**. Walt, is that you?

**WALT**. You…boo!

**HARRIET**. Go away Walt.

> (**WALT** *begins to knock harder.*)

**HARRIET**. *Walt! Go away! We're busy!*

**WALT**. Busy…

**NANCY**. Walt! Come here honey!

**WALT**. *(as he exits)* Honey…bunny!

**HARRIET**. Thanks, mom! Louanne, you look beautiful in that dress!

**LOUANNE**. Do you really think so?

**HARRIET**. Absolutely! Now, let me get some shoes.

**LOUANNE**. But I don't want to use all of your good things, Harriet!

**HARRIET**. I already have my outfit picked out. I love doing this!

**LOUANNE**. If you're sure…

**HARRIET**. I'm sure. Here, try these on. *(She hands her some shoes.)*

> (**LOUANNE** *puts on the shoes. They have heels, and* **LOUANNE** *walks very carefully so she doesn't fall over. She puts her arms straight out to the sides and looks down as if she is walking across a rope.*)

**LOUANNE**. I never wear heels, Harriet.

**HARRIET**. I can see that. Here. Look up and put your arms down.

(**WALT** *has returned and he uses a loud object to knock on the door. It scares* **LOUANNE** *and she falls over.*)

**LOUANNE.** Whoa! What was that?

**HARRIET.** Are you all right, Louanne?

**LOUANNE.** I'm fine. *(gets up and brushes herself off)* What *was* that?

**HARRIET.** It's Walt trying to knock down my door.

**WALT.** Door…four!

(**WALT** *begins to open the door.*)

**HARRIET.** No!

(**HARRIET** *closes the door.* **WALT** *tries to open it.*)

**LOUANNE.** He sure can rhyme!

**WALT.** Rhyme…time!

**LOUANNE.** Maybe we should just let him in.

**HARRIET.** No! He'll just ruin everything. *MOM! Walt is bugging us again!*

**NANCY.** Walter! Come and brush your teeth!

(**WALT** *exits.*)

**HARRIET.** *(She peeks out her door and sees that* **WALT** *is gone.)* Saved by good dental health! *(beat)* Do you want to see my dance?

**LOUANNE.** Sure!

(**HARRIET** *winds up her snow globe.*)

**LOUANNE.** Isn't that the snow globe that your mom gave you when you were born?

**HARRIET.** Yes. It's my favorite thing in the whole world. I still remember how mom used to sing me to sleep with it. No matter how sad I felt, when I heard her voice I always knew that everything would be O.K. *(beat)* The problem is, Walt loves it. Every time he hears it, he tries to get in my room and dance with me.

**LOUANNE.** That's pretty cute, Harriet.

**HARRIET.** I guess. But he sure can be a pest.

### *SONG No. 3: SNOW GLOBE LULLABY*

*(HARRIET begins her ballet. Lights shift. On another part of the stage, lights come up on NANCY holding HARRIET when she was a baby. NANCY sings a lullaby to baby HARRIET.)*

**NANCY.**
SLEEP PRETTY HARRIET, DON'T YOU CRY,
JUST LISTEN TO THIS SNOW GLOBE LULLABY.
SWEET DREAMS WILL BE HERE WITH YOU WHILE YOU SLEEP,
AND THIS MEM'RY OF YOU I SHALL ALWAYS KEEP.

HERE THE WORLD IS SAFE AND WHITE,
TO GIVE YOU SWEET DREAMS THROUGHOUT THE NIGHT.
SNOW GLOBE LULLABY
IT'S TIME TO CLOSE YOUR EYES.
HUSH NOW, DARLING, BABY DON'T YOU CRY.

*(Snow globe lighting effect as in opening. BALLERINA enters and dances.)*

HUSH, LET THE MELODY SOOTHE YOUR MIND,
MAY ALL OF YOUR THOUGHTS BE PEACEFUL AND KIND.
I WILL BE WITH YOU YOUR WHOLE LIFE LONG,
TO SING YOU THIS LULLABY SONG,
TO SING YOU THIS LULLABY SONG.

**CHORUS.**
HERE THE WORLD IS SAFE AND WHITE,
TO GIVE YOU SWEET DREAMS THROUGHOUT THE NIGHT.
SNOW GLOBE LULLABY,
IT'S TIME TO CLOSE YOUR EYES,
HUSH NOW, DARLING, BABY DON'T YOU CRY.

*(Lights shift back to HARRIET as she finishes her dance. WALT has found a loud horn which he blows outside the door.)*

**LOUANNE & HARRIET.** *(startled)* Aughhh!

**HARRIET.** *Mom! Walt is driving us crazy!*

**WALT.** Crazy…lazy!

*(WALT opens the door. HARRIET closes it. WALT keeps trying to open it. HARRIET sits down and holds door closed with the bottoms of her feet.)*

**HARRIET.** *Mom! Save me! Walt is ruining my life and the lives of others!*

**NANCY.** *(enters)* What's all this noise?

(**HARRIET** *opens door.*)

**HARRIET.** We're trying to have a sleepover and Walt won't leave us alone!

**NANCY.** *(enters* **HARRIET***'s room and sees* **LOUANNE***)* Well Louanne! Don't you look pretty! Are you going to wear that dress to the Winter Carnival?

**LOUANNE.** If it's all right.

**NANCY.** Of course it is! It looks lovely on you!

(**WALT** *sneaks in and moves towards the snow globe and tries to take it.*)

**HARRIET.** Mom! Walt is trying to get my snow globe!

**NANCY.** No, Walt. That's Harriet's special snow globe.

**WALT.** Globe…

*(He does a little dance turn.)*

**LOUANNE.** Awww! How cute!

**HARRIET.** Cute…

**NANCY.** Come on, Walt. It's time for bed.

**WALT.** *(Starts to cry.)*

**NANCY.** Well, good night girls.

**HARRIET.** Good night mom. Night, Walt.

**LOUANNE.** Good night!

(**WALT**, *still crying, runs over to* **HARRIET** *and gives her a hug.* **HARRIET** *hugs him back.*)

**HARRIET.** Sweet dreams, Walt.

(**HARRIET** *smiles at* **WALT**. *He stops crying and exits with* **NANCY**.)

**NANCY.** You're a good sister, Harriet.

*(They exit.)*

**LOUANNE.** Wow! How did you do that?

**HARRIET.** I don't know. But usually after I give him a good night hug he'll go to bed.

**LOUANNE.** He sure loves you.

**HARRIET.** Yeah. I just wish he didn't want to be with me every second.

**LOUANNE.** I'm sure it gets old, but I think it would be fun to have a little brother or sister. It's so sweet how Walt wants to be with you all the time.

**HARRIET.** Yeah, sweet. Want some more popcorn?

**LOUANNE.** Do you really need to ask?

*(They laugh, throw popcorn up in the air and catch it in their mouths. They continue talking as lights fade on scene.)*

*(**No. 3A Scene Shift** music plays into the next scene.)*

## Scene Three

*(The next afternoon.* **HARRIET** *is mixing cookie batter in a big bowl.* **NANCY** *is folding clothes.* **KIDS** *are outside.)*

**NANCY.** You girls certainly sounded like you had fun last night!

**HARRIET.** We did. Can I take some of these cookies to my friends? I'm going to meet them outside and practice for the Winter Carnival.

**NANCY.** What are you going to practice today?

**HARRIET.** The snowman building race, sledding, best snow angel…everything!

**NANCY.** Sounds fun, Harriet!

**HARRIET.** I think they're already outside!

*(***HARRIET*** looks out the window.* **WALT** *sneaks into the kitchen. He has* **HARRIET***'s snow globe. He walks over to the cookie bowl and begins to eat some batter.* **NANCY** *and* **HARRIET** *don't notice him.)*

See! There they are! *Everyone* is out there, mom! Can I go? *Please?*

**NANCY.** After you finish baking the cookies, dear. It's important to finish what you start.

*(***AUNT SUSAN*** enters.* ***No. 3B Hawaiian Music Underscore*** *plays. She is dressed in a Hawaiian outfit. She does a little hula dance as she calls* **NANCY***. Phone rings.)*

**NANCY.** Hello?

**SUSAN.** Aloha, Nancy! It's your favorite sister!

**NANCY.** *(***NANCY*** laughs.)* My *only* sister! Aloha, Susan!

*(***HARRIET*** rushes over to* **NANCY***.)*

**HARRIET.** *(excited)* Aunt Susan? Is she still in Hawaii? Is she going to work at the Winter Carnival again this year?

**NANCY.** *(to* **HARRIET***)* Yes, honey. Shhh. *(to* **SUSAN***)* How are you, Susan?

**SUSAN.** Just wonderful! Hawaii is so beautiful!

**NANCY.** Oh, I wish I was there with you!

**HARRIET.** When will she be here?

*(NANCY signals for HARRIET to be quiet.)*

**SUSAN.** Me too. Next time, you promise?

**NANCY.** I promise! So, are you still coming for a visit?

**SUSAN.** Of course! I'll be there tomorrow night!

**NANCY.** Wonderful! We can't wait to see you!

**SUSAN.** Me too! See you soon! Kisses to Harriet and Walt! Bye!

**NANCY.** Bye!

*(AUNT SUSAN closes her phone and exits doing the hula. NANCY puts away her phone.)*

*(WALT is still eating cookie batter.)*

**HARRIET.** When's she coming?

**NANCY.** She'll be here tomorrow night!

**HARRIET.** Hurray! I can't wait! I just love it when Aunt Susan visits!

**WALT.** Hurray!

*(HARRIET and NANCY see WALT with cookie batter on his face and holding the snow globe.)*

**HARRIET.** *Oh no! MOM! Walt is eating the cookie dough!* And *he has my snow globe!*

**NANCY.** *WALT! NO!*

*(NANCY walks towards WALT. WALT drops the bowl of batter and runs from her. HARRIET begins to chase WALT. Chase scene.)*

**HARRIET.** Don't drop my snow globe, Walt! I'll never forgive you if you break it!

**NANCY.** Walt! Stop running!

**WALT.** Wheee! *(He continues to run.)*

**HARRIET.** Mom! *Do* something!

**NANCY.** *(NANCY begins to sing:)*

FREEZE LIKE A STATUE, A STATUE, A STATUE,
FREEZE LIKE A STATUE, DON'T YOU MOVE!

*(They all freeze in place.)*

**HARRIET.** Where'd you learn that?

**NANCY.** A "Mommy and Me" class we took. Harriet, don't move. *(speaking very sweetly:)* Walt, if you bring Mommy the snow globe, I'll give you a treat.

**HARRIET.** Great. Let's reward Walt for robbery.

**NANCY.** Hush, Harriet. I'm trying to get your snow globe back in one piece. Desperate times require...oh, never mind.

*(WALT slowly walks to NANCY and hands her the snow globe. HARRIET and NANCY hold their "freeze" poses until the snow globe is safely in NANCY's hands. HARRIET runs to inspect it.)*

**HARRIET.** Is my snow globe all right? It's not broken is it?

**NANCY.** No it's not broken, dear. Just a little sticky. You need to be sure and put it up higher so he can't reach it.

**HARRIET.** Don't worry, I will. And now I don't have any cookies to take to my friends. Great. May I go now?

**NANCY.** I suppose. We can make cookies another time.

*(NANCY gives WALT a treat and then begins to clean up. WALT tries to "help.")*

*(HARRIET puts her snow globe in a safe place. She gets her coat, etc. and starts to get ready to go outside.)*

**HARRIET.** *(under her breath)* Sometimes I wish that I didn't even have a brother!

*(HARRIET is ready to go outside.)*

Bye Mom!

**NANCY.** Harriet! Don't forget Walt!

**HARRIET.** WHAT?

**NANCY.** I said, don't forget Walt. I need to clean the guest room for Aunt Susan. I'll get his coat on. Come on, Walt.

*(NANCY and WALT exit.)*

**HARRIET.** Oh great! I suppose I'll have to take him to the Winter Carnival too! My life is over!

### *SONG No. 4: DON'T FORGET WALT*

**HARRIET.**

DON'T FORGET WALT, THAT'S ALL I EVER HEAR.
WHY HE'S GOT TO BE WITH ME JUST ISN'T VERY CLEAR.
WHEN I WANT ALONE TIME, A MOMENT JUST FOR ME,
MY MOM SAYS, "TAKE YOUR BROTHER!"
WHY CAN'T HE JUST LET ME BE?

DON'T FORGET WALT, HE'S A NUISANCE, HE'S A PEST,
HOW CAN I FORGET? HE DOESN'T GIVE ME ANY REST.
WHEN I WANT TO DRESS UP OR PLAY WITH MY FAV'RITE TOY,
THE LAST THING THAT I WANT AROUND IS A LITTLE BOY!

HE IS LITTLE, HE IS SWEET.
BUT I'M FEELING REALLY BEAT.
SOMETIMES IT'S LIKE MY OWN MOM DOESN'T CARE.
HE'S MY BROTHER, THIS IS TRUE,
BUT HE STICKS TO ME LIKE GLUE!
I JUST WANT TO WASH HIM RIGHT OUT OF MY HAIR,
WHY CAN'T I JUST WASH HIM RIGHT OUT OF MY HAIR?
FOR ONCE AND FOR ALL JUST TO WASH HIM RIGHT OUT OF MY HAIR!

(**NANCY** *enters with* **WALT**. **KIDS** *come onstage.*)

(*spoken:*)

**NANCY.** Walt is all ready, dear. Thank you for watching him. Will you be warm enough? It looks cold out today!

**HARRIET.** I'm fine, mom. Except for that fact that I have to take Walt everywhere!

**NANCY.** *(not really paying attention)* That's nice dear.

**HARRIET.** Nice? What would be nice is a day by MYSELF!

**NANCY.** All right, dear. I really must go and start cleaning. Don't...

**HARRIET.** *I KNOW, I KNOW!!! YOU DON'T NEED TO SAY IT!*

*VOCALS:*

**HARRIET.**
> DON'T FORGET WALT, YOU'D THINK BY NOW THAT SHE WOULD SEE

**KIDS.**
> DON'T FORGET WALT, YOU'D THINK BY NOW THAT SHE WOULD SEE

**HARRIET.**
> THIS REALLY ISN'T WORKING, NOT FOR HIM AND NOT FOR ME.

**KIDS.**
> HE'S REALLY SUCH A DARLING, JUST AS CUTE AS HE CAN BE

**HARRIET.**
> I TRY TO DO MY BEST

**KIDS.**
> SHE TRIES TO DO HER BEST,

**HARRIET.**
> BUT IT'S REALLY NOT MY FAULT.

**KIDS.**
> BUT WHO CAN BLAME HER?

**HARRIET.**
> 'CAUSE THEN HE STARTS TO DRIVE ME CRAZY,
> AND THEN HE KEEPS DRIVING ME CRAZY,
> I'M GONNA GO CRAZY IF I DON'T FORGET
> ALL ABOUT WALT!

**KIDS.**
> DON'T FORGET WALT!
> DON'T FORGET WALT!
> DON'T FORGET! (YOU BETTER NOT!)
> DON'T FORGET! (YOU BETTER NOT!)
>
> *(The following lines are spoken simultaneously, in rhythm :)*

**KIDS.**
> DON'T FORGET, DON'T FORGET, DON'T FORGET, DON'T FORGET
> YOU BETTER NOT, BETTER NOT, BETTER NOT FORGET

**HARRIET.**
>PLEASE, PLEASE, PLEASE, LET ME JUST FORGET
>
>(**WALT** *has found the snow globe and picks it up.* **HARRIET** *reacts :)*

**HARRIET.** *(shout)*
>WAAAAALT!!!

**KIDS.** *(shout)*
>WALT!
>
>*(**No. 4A DON'T FORGET WALT** Playoff/Scene Shift music plays into the next scene.)*

## Scene Four

(***DON'T FORGET WALT*** *music plays as* **HARRIET** *and* **WALT** *join* **KIDS** *outside.*)

**LOUANNE.** Hi Harriet! Hi Walt! How are you doing?

**HARRIET.** I'm O.K. I have to watch Walt again though. Life is so unfair. You didn't start without me, did you?

**GEORGE.** Just getting ready.

**ARNIE.** Hi Walt!

**WALT.** Arnie…Barney!

**ARNIE.** He sure seems happy all the time.

**HARRIET.** Sure, *he's* happy.

(**WALT** *hugs* **HARRIET**)

**TINA.** That is so cute!

**GEORGE.** *(sarcastically)* Yeah. Cute.

**OSWALDO.** Walt reminds me of when I was a youngster. One day I was walking home from school after a huge snowstorm. I could hardly see in front of me when suddenly I remembered…

**LOUANNE.** Remembered what?

**OSWALDO.** Oh, it really isn't important. The past *is* the past.

(**SYDNEY** *enters with a very unusual looking machine – obviously homemade. It has a weather vane on top and many pieces that can spin and move.*)

**SYDNEY.** Hello!

**ALL.** *(staggered)* Sydney! Hi! We're glad you're here! *(etc.)*

**ARNIE.** What's that, Sydney?

**SYDNEY.** This is my latest invention. Besides being able to check the temperature, air pressure, humidity, speed and direction of the wind, it can also estimate the amount of snow needed to make the biggest and most stable snowman under the existing weather conditions.

**KIDS.** Wow!

**TINA.** How does it work?

**SYDNEY.** As you probably know, snowflakes are loose clusters of ice crystals usually with a flat, six-sided shape.

**TINA.** A hexagon!

**SYDNEY.** Very good, Tina! Now, this thermometer measures the water vapor in the air. Naturally when the temperature is lower, there is less water vapor so the crystals tend to be smaller.

**OSWALDO.** Do we want them smaller?

**SYDNEY.** No. We prefer larger ice crystals thus giving us more snow to create the ideal snowman. *(She points to another part of her machine.)* This of course is a weather vane. This way we will know precisely where the wind is coming from.

**GEORGE.** How will that help anything?

**SYDNEY.** Once we know from where the strongest winds are blowing, we can place some of us in a position to block it from the snowman.

**LOUANNE.** Good thinking, Sydney!

**SYDNEY.** Thank you.

**ARNIE.** *(pointing)* What about this?

**GEORGE.** Looks like a slushy maker!

*(They all laugh.)*

**SYDNEY.** Actually, it's a timer. That way I can help build the snowman without having to use the stop watch.

**LOUANNE.** Wow, Sydney! You *are* a genius.

**SYDNEY.** Thank you. I believe it's important to make good use of our brains.

**WALT.** *(He has been sneaking over to see the machine.)* BRAIN… PAIN!

*(He scares **SYDNEY**, and she accidentally spins some of the controls on her machine which makes sounds. A part may fall off.)*

**SYDNEY.** Aughh!

**GEORGE.** *(giving **WALT** a dirty look)* Speaking of pain…

**TINA.** Don't be mean, George.

**GEORGE.** Well, I don't want to do all of this work and then have Walt knock over our snowman again.

**HARRIET.** Don't worry, George. I have an idea. Come on, Walt.

*(She takes his hand and leads him to the flagpole.)*

Walt, you need to stay here for a few minutes. This is a very important pole. It's holding up the American flag. You need to watch the flag for me, O.K.? Don't move from this spot! And Walt, whatever you do, don't put your tongue on that flagpole, do you understand?

**WALT.** Pole...hole.

**HARRIET.** I'll take that as a yes. *(She runs to her friends.)*

**SYDNEY.** On your mark, get set...

**HARRIET.** I'm ready!

**SYDNEY.** Go!

### *SONG No. 5: THE SNOWMAN RACE*

**KIDS.**
> FIRST WE MAKE A SNOWBALL, THEN PACK IT TIGHT.
> THEN WE MAKE IT BIGGER, SUCH A LOVELY SIGHT.
> WE NEED TO WORK TOGETHER, IT'S THE ONLY WAY
> TO WIN THE SNOWMAN RACE AND THEN WE'LL HEAR
>    THEM SAY:

> NOW THAT'S A SNOWMAN!
> HE'S THE BEST!
> A ROCKIN' SNOWMAN!
> HE'LL PASS THE TEST!
> NO THERE AIN'T NO BETTER SNOWMAN THAT WE CAN SEE,
> IT ALL CAME TOGETHER SO EASILY,
> HE'S GOT THE HEAD, THE BODY AND OH THAT FACE,
> WE JUST HOPE THE TEAM CAN WIN
> THE SNOWMAN RACE!

> NEXT WE MAKE THE BODY, SO JOLLY AND ROUND.
> PLACE IT CAREFULLY ON THE SOFT SNOWY GROUND.
> NEXT WE MAKE THE HEAD, A NOSE, A MOUTH AND TWO EYES.
> AND IF WE'VE DONE IT FAST ENOUGH WE'LL WIN THE
>    PRIZE!

NOW THAT'S A SNOWMAN!
HE'S THE BEST!
A ROCKING SNOWMAN!
HE'LL PASS THE TEST!
NO THERE AIN'T NO BETTER SNOWMAN THAT WE CAN SEE,
IT ALL CAME TOGETHER SO EASILY,
HE'S GOT THE HEAD, THE BODY AND OH THAT FACE,
WE JUST HOPE THE TEAM CAN WIN
(PLEASE, PLEASE, PLEASE, PLEASE, PLEASE LET US WIN!)
THE SNOWMAN RACE!

*(Dance break as the **KIDS** finish building the snowman.)*

NOW THAT'S A SNOWMAN!
HE'S THE BEST!
A ROCKING SNOWMAN!
HE'LL PASS THE TEST!
NO THERE AIN'T NO BETTER SNOWMAN THAT WE CAN SEE,
IT ALL CAME TOGETHER SO EASILY,
HE'S GOT THE HEAD, THE BODY AND OH THAT FACE,
WE JUST HOPE THE TEAM CAN WIN

(PLEASE, PLEASE, PLEASE, PLEASE, PLEASE LET US WIN!)
THE SNOWMAN RACE!
THE SNOWMAN RACE!
THE SNOWMAN RACE!
THE SNOWMAN RACE!
YEAH!

*(In the beginning of the song, **WALT** watches the flag intently. He salutes the flag and marches around the pole. After a while he gets bored and becomes curious about the flagpole. He sticks out his tongue a few times towards the pole. He is about to touch his tongue to the flagpole toward the end of the song when **HARRIET** notices him.)*

**HARRIET.** *WALT, NO!!!*

*(She runs to **WALT**. **KIDS** follow.)*

**WALT.** *(**HARRIET**'s yell scares him and he begins to cry.)* WHAAAA! WHAAAA! *(continues crying)*

**HARRIET.** Are you all right?

**GEORGE.** Way to go, Walt! You almost got yourself stuck to the pole. *(He laughs.)*

**HARRIET.** Be quiet George! This isn't funny!

*(She hugs* **WALT**. **WALT** *stops crying.)*

**LOUANNE.** Do you know how much that would have hurt?

**ARNIE.** I had a friend who put his tongue on a pole and he had to go to the hospital. It took a long time for his tongue to heal.

**OSWALDO.** *(a bit defensively)* Do we really need to talk about that right now?

**ARNIE.** I didn't mean *you*, Oswaldo.

**OSWALDO.** Oh. *(beat)*

**SYDNEY.** The important thing is that Walt didn't make contact. Well done, Harriet.

**NANCY.** *(calls outside)* Harriet! Walt! Time to come inside!

**HARRIET.** Got to go everyone! See you later!

**ALL.** *(staggered)* Bye Harriet! Bye Walt! See you soon! *(etc.)*

*(**No. 5A THE SNOWMAN RACE** Scene Shift music plays.)*

## Scene Five

*(The day before the Winter Carnival.* **HARRIET**'s **AUNT SUSAN** *and* **NANCY** *are talking in* **NANCY**'s *house).*

SUSAN. I can't wait to surprise Harriet and Walt!

NANCY. They are so excited to see you! All I've been hearing from Harriet is: "When will Aunt Susan be here? What time does she fly in? Is she here yet?"

SUSAN. So the kids really don't know that I'm here early?

NANCY. No. They still think that you're coming tonight.

*(NANCY gets up and looks out the window.)*

SUSAN. Wonderful! When will they be here?

NANCY. They should be back any minute. I sent them to the store for some puppy chow.

SUSAN. Good thinking!

NANCY. Oh! Here they come! Hide!

SUSAN. Where should I hide?

NANCY. How about behind the chair?

*(SUSAN "hides" behind the chair, but can easily be seen.)*

Uh, no. Bad idea. Under the table! Quick!

*(SUSAN "hides" under the table, but again can be seen.)*

SUSAN. How about behind the sofa?

NANCY. Good thinking, big sister!

*(SUSAN hides behind sofa just as* **HARRIET** *and* **WALT** *come in.* **HARRIET** *is carrying a bag half full of puppy chow.)*

NANCY. *(looking at bag)* Harriet?

HARRIET. Yes, mom?

NANCY. What happened to the bag of puppy chow?

HARRIET. We got hungry.

NANCY. I see. Let's unbundle you, Walt.

*(NANCY tries to help WALT take off his coat but he runs away from her. NANCY starts to chase him, but WALT*

*runs behind the sofa. Not wanting* **HARRIET** *to see* **SUSAN**, **NANCY** *quickly walks to* **HARRIET** *and helps to take off her coat.)*

**HARRIET.** I got it, mom. Thanks.

*(***WALT*** begins to giggle behind the sofa.)*

**WALT.** Hurray!

**HARRIET.** What is he doing back there? *(***HARRIET*** begins to cross to sofa.)*

**NANCY.** *(***NANCY*** stops* **HARRIET** *and desperately tries to divert her attention.)* Nothing! Let's have some puppy chow!

*(***NANCY*** grabs the puppy chow and begins to eat some.)*

**HARRIET.** *(Looks at* **NANCY** *strangely.)* But I'm not hungry anymore. *(beat)* Are you stressed again, mom?

**NANCY.** Stressed? No! I'm not stressed! Just a little hungry!

*(***NANCY*** keeps eating.)*

*(***WALT***'s scarf, hat, etc. are thrown up in the air behind sofa.)*

**WALT.** Wheee!!!

**HARRIET.** What is he...

*(***HARRIET*** crosses to sofa. As she gets closer,* **NANCY** *pushes her onto the sofa and sits down next to her.)*

**NANCY.** *(offers* **HARRIET** *some puppy chow)* Are you sure you aren't hungry?

**HARRIET.** Yes mom! I mean no, I'm not! What's going on? You're acting so weird! And don't you want to know what Walt is doing back there?

*(***HARRIET*** starts to look behind sofa.* **NANCY** *pulls her back.)*

**WALT.** Hee hee hee!!!

**NANCY.** Who?

**HARRIET.** Walt! Your son.

**NANCY.** Oh, him. I'm sure he's fine. I just think that this would be a good time for us to talk about college!

**HARRIET.** College?! But I'm not even in High School yet!

(**WALT** *comes out from behind sofa. He is wearing a flowered shirt and a hula skirt over his clothes. He's grinning and begins to do the hula.*)

**WALT.** Shhh! Secret...cricket!

**HARRIET.** Secret cricket? What? How? Where did he get a Hawaiian skirt? And why are you both acting like this???

(**AUNT SUSAN** *gets up from behind the sofa.*)

**AUNT SUSAN.** Surprise!!!

**HARRIET.** Aunt Susan!

(**HARRIET** *runs over to* **SUSAN** *and they hug.*)

**SUSAN.** Hello, Harriet! Are you surprised?

**HARRIET.** Surprised and relieved! I thought mom and Walt were cracking up! *(They laugh.)*

**NANCY.** I didn't know what to do when Walt ran behind the sofa!

**HARRIET.** *(to* **SUSAN***)* I didn't think that you were going to be here until tonight!

**SUSAN.** I was able to get an earlier flight! *(beat)* I'm so happy to see you! Look how much you've grown! Oh, I have a shirt for you too!

(**SUSAN** *takes a shirt and lei out of a bag for* **HARRIET** *and* **NANCY**.)

**HARRIET.** Thank you! They're beautiful!

**NANCY.** How thoughtful, Susan!

**SUSAN.** I have a grass skirt for you too Harriet, but I'm afraid that I had to put it on Walt to keep him quiet.

**WALT.** Quiet...buy it!

**NANCY.** Walt is learning to rhyme.

**SUSAN.** Very good, Walt!

**WALT.** Walt...salt!

**SUSAN.** That's great!

**WALT.** Great...late!

**SUSAN.** Wow!

**WALT.** Wow…pow!

**HARRIET.** The problem is, once he gets started, he doesn't like to stop.

**WALT.** Stop…pop!

**NANCY.** Walt, it's time for your nap.

**WALT.** Nap…snap!

**NANCY.** Say goodbye to Aunt Susan!

**WALT.** *(He runs to* **SUSAN** *and hugs her.)* Bye…fly!

**SUSAN.** Have a nice nap, Walt! I love you!

**WALT.** Love you!

*(***WALT*** runs to ***HARRIET*** and gives her a hug.)*

**HARRIET.** Love you, Walt.

**WALT.** *(to* **HARRIET***)* Love you!

**NANCY.** I'll be right back.

*(***NANCY*** takes ***WALT****'s hand and leads him to his room.)*

*(***WALT*** waves goodbye.)*

**SUSAN.** You're a good big sister, Harriet.

**HARRIET.** Thanks. I try to be, but sometimes it is so hard! I feel like I *always* have to watch Walt when all I want to do is be with my friends.

**SUSAN.** I know exactly what you mean, Harriet.

**HARRIET.** You do?

**SUSAN.** Sure! Your mom used to follow me everywhere! I remember how she always wanted to play with my favorite doll. Her name was Dollie. Hmmm…apparently I wasn't very original as a child. *(beat)* Anyway, Dollie had long beautiful ringlets and real eyelashes. My mother even made us matching dresses. I had to hide her so your mom couldn't find her. But one day…

*(Lights change and **No. 5B YOUNG SUSAN AND YOUNG NANCY** plays as* **SUSAN** *continues to "tell"* **HARRIET** *the story. Two* **GIRLS** *act out the following:)*

**YOUNG SUSAN.** Give Dollie back to me, Nancy!

**YOUNG NANCY.** *(chasing* **YOUNG NANCY***)* Dollie! Dollie!

**YOUNG SUSAN.** She's mine! I share everything with you! But not Dollie! Give her back right now!

**YOUNG NANCY.** Dollie! Dollie! *(Dollie's head falls off.)*

**YOUNG SUSAN.** Oh no, Nancy! Look what you did! You broke her head off!

**YOUNG NANCY.** Uh-oh… *(She picks up Dollie's head.)*

**YOUNG SUSAN.** Mom!!! Nancy broke Dollie!

*(She cries and runs off followed by* **YOUNG NANCY.***)*

*(Lights shift back.)*

**HARRIET.** I'll bet you were really mad.

**SUSAN.** I sure was! Even though my mom was able to put Dollie's head back on, I was still angry at your mom. But soon after that something really bad happened.

**HARRIET.** What?

**SUSAN.** It was winter, and we went ice skating with my friends. Your mom wandered off and ended up on some very thin ice. The second I saw her and yelled her name, the ice cracked and Nancy fell through. We all rushed to her, and I was able to throw her my scarf and pull her out. It was the scariest moment of my life. *(beat)* The first thing that I did when we got home was to give her Dollie.

**HARRIET.** Mom never told me that story!

**SUSAN.** Really? Well, maybe she didn't want to scare you. *(beat)* Anyway Harriet, that accident changed our relationship forever. Even though she still followed me everywhere, I realized it was because she just wanted to be like me.

*(***NANCY*** enters.)*

Now we have a relationship that will last our lifetimes. I don't know what I'd do without her.

**NANCY.** Without who?

**SUSAN.** You, little sister! Of course we didn't *always* get along.

**NANCY.** That's true. Susan did like to play jokes on her innocent baby sister.

**SUSAN.** Ha! I believe that you irritated me on more than one occasion!

**NANCY.** *(innocently)* Who *me?*

**SUSAN.** Yes, *you!* Remember when you hid my bicycle?

**NANCY.** It wasn't for long! Besides, you unstuffed my stuffed cat!

**SUSAN.** It was old! You put soap on my toothbrush!

**NANCY.** Did not!

**SUSAN.** Did too!

**NANCY.** Did not!

**SUSAN.** Too!

**NANCY.** Not!

### *SONG No. 6: WHAT WOULD I DO WITHOUT YOU?*

**SUSAN.**
>WHEN WE WERE SO MUCH YOUNGER

**NANCY.**
>WE'D BOTH PLAY HIDE AND SEEK,
>I'D CLOSE MY EYES AND COUNT TO TEN

**SUSAN.**
>AND YOU WOULD ALWAYS PEEK!

**NANCY.** *(spoken)*
>Did not!

**SUSAN.** *(spoken)*
>Did too!

**NANCY.**
>YOU READ MY SECRET DIARY,
>AND THREW AWAY THE KEY,

**SUSAN.**
>YOU BORROWED MY BEST SWEATER,
>AND I FOUND IT IN A TREE!
>BUT NOW THAT WE ARE OLDER, WE ARE THE BEST OF FRIENDS.
>THE MEMORIES AND LOVE WE SHARE ARE NEVER GOING TO END.

**BOTH.**
> WHAT WOULD I DO WITHOUT YOU MY SISTER?
> WHAT WOULD I DO WITHOUT YOUR SMILE?
> WHAT WOULD I DO WITHOUT YOU MY BEST FRIEND?
> WHAT WOULD I DO? WHAT WOULD I DO?
> WHAT WOULD I DO WITHOUT YOU?

**SUSAN.**
> YOU TIED MY SHOES TOGETHER.

**NANCY.**
> YOU BROKE MY FAVORITE CHAIR.

**SUSAN.**
> YOU LOCKED ME IN THE BASEMENT.

**NANCY.**
> YOU CUT OFF ALL MY HAIR.

**SUSAN.** *(spoken)* It looked cute short!

**NANCY.**
> YOU FLUSHED MY COIN COLLECTION,
> ALL I COULD DO WAS CRY,

**SUSAN.**
> YOU DROPPED A FISH INTO MY BATH,
> I THOUGHT THAT I WOULD DIE!

**NANCY.**
> BUT EVEN THOUGH WE'RE OLDER, YOU'RE STILL MY BRIGHTEST STAR,
> AND EVEN THOUGH WE'RE FAR APART, I STILL LIKE BEING WHERE YOU ARE.

**SUSAN.**
> I STILL LIKE BEING WHERE YOU ARE.

**BOTH.**
> WHAT WOULD I DO WITHOUT YOU MY SISTER?
> WHAT WOULD I DO WITHOUT YOUR SMILE?
> WHAT WOULD I DO WITHOUT YOU MY BEST FRIEND?
> WHAT WOULD I DO? WHAT WOULD I DO?
> WHAT WOULD I DO WITHOUT YOU?
> WITHOUT YOU?

*(SUSAN and NANCY hug.)*

**HARRIET.** Wow. I never realized. I mean, I guess I never think about you and my mom as being young...I mean, like me...you know what I mean.

*(*SUSAN *and* NANCY *laugh.)*

**SUSAN.** I do, Harriet. But we were your age once, and we did feel all of those things.

**NANCY.** Having a sister or a brother is very special, Harriet. And in our case, it's just gotten better through the years.

**SUSAN.** Now, tell me about tomorrow! What team are you on and what are you going to do first?

**HARRIET.** We're the red team. First there is the Snow Angel Race. Then the Snowman Race. We've really been practicing for that. Then the Sled Race begins. I'm not going to do that, but it's really fun to watch. Next we will...

*(***HARRIET** *continues to talk about the next day as lights fade.* ***No. 6A WHAT WOULD I DO WITHOUT YOU?*** *Scene Shift music.)*

## Scene Six

*(The Winter Carnival. All the **KIDS**, **AUNT SUSAN** & **NANCY** are there. **AUNT SUSAN** is announcing the games. There is much excitement and activity as the **KIDS** are warming up for the Snow Angel Race. Some are running in place, doing yoga, stretching, etc. **GEORGE**, **OSWALDO** & **LOUANNE** are the first ones to "race.")*

**SUSAN.** Welcome to the Winter Carnival! Will the first group please get into places for the Snow Angel Race? Thank you. Remember, you will have ten seconds to make your best snow angel. Ready? On your mark, get set, go!

*(**GEORGE**, **OSWALDO** & **LOUANNE** make snow angels.)*

**ALL.** *(staggered)* Come on, you can do it! Flap your arms but not too fast! Good leg action! Hurry! *(etc.)*

*(**SUSAN** blows whistle. **GEORGE**, **OSWALDO** and **LOUANNE** stand. **SUSAN** "listens" to the voice in her headset.)*

**SUSAN.** And the winner is…Oswaldo!

*(**OSWALDO** is stunned.)*

**ALL.** *(staggered)* Good job, Oswaldo! Way to go! You deserved it! Good try, Louanne! *("George," etc. **KIDS** clap and cheer.)*

**OSWALDO.** I won? Really? I won! Did you guys hear that? I finally *won* something! After all these years of being frozen with fear, and now…I actually WON!

**GEORGE.** Yeah, great. But remember, it's only a Snow Angel Race. It's not like you won a sledding race or something.

**OSWALDO.** Thanks for the validation, George.

**GEORGE.** Anytime.

**SUSAN.** Group number two! Please take your positions!

*(**HARRIET**, **ARNIE**, **TINA** & **SYDNEY** prepare for the Snow Angel Race.)*

**SUSAN.** On your mark, get set, go!

**ALL.** *(staggered)* Go Harriet *("ARNIE, TINA, SYDNEY!")* You can do it! Stay focused! *(etc.)*

*(As the race is taking place, **WALT** wanders over to **HARRIET**. Before anyone can react, he lies right next to **HARRIET** and begins to make a snow angel. It ruins **HARRIET**'s snow angel. Some laughter, some "aww's" from friends.)*

*(**SUSAN** blows her whistle.)*

**GEORGE.** Oh great! Walt is going to make Harriet lose!

**NANCY.** Walt, honey, come here!

*(**SUSAN** "listens" to the voice in her headset as before.)*

**SUSAN.** And the winner is....Tina!

**ALL.** *(staggered)* Hurray! Way to go Tina! *(Some clapping and cheering, etc.)*

**HARRIET.** Thanks a lot, Walt.

*(She takes his hand and leads him over to **NANCY**.)*

**SUSAN.** And now it's time for the Snowman Race!

**ARNIE.** The Snowman Race!

*(**KIDS** take their position to build the snowman.)*

**KIDS.** *(staggered)* Here we go! We can do this! Come on everyone! *(etc.)*

**GEORGE.** We've just got to win this one.

**TINA.** Come on, team!

**SYDNEY.** Remember, work together and don't forget that we only need to cut down our time by 3 seconds!

**KIDS.** *(staggered)* All right! We can do it! You know it! *(etc.)*

**SUSAN.** On your mark, get set, go!

### *SONG No. 7: THE SNOWMAN RACE (REPRISE)*

*(Kids build snowman. Shouting, cheering, etc. After snowman is completed, they sing:)*

**CHORUS.**
NOW THAT'S A SNOWMAN!
HE'S THE BEST!
A ROCKIN' SNOWMAN!
HE'LL PASS THE TEST!

NO THERE AIN'T NO BETTER SNOWMAN THAT WE CAN SEE,
IT ALL CAME TOGETHER SO EASILY!
HE'S GOT THE HEAD, THE BODY AND OH THAT FACE,
WE JUST HOPE THE TEAM CAN WIN
(PLEASE, PLEASE, PLEASE, PLEASE, PLEASE LET US WIN!)
THE SNOWMAN RACE! THE SNOWMAN RACE!
THE SNOWMAN RACE! THE SNOWMAN RACE!
YEAH!

*(At the end of the Snowman Race,* **WALT** *runs over to* **HARRIET** *and gives her a big hug which knocks her over.)*

*(***SUSAN*** blows her whistle.)*

**SUSAN.** And the winner is... *(a little disappointed)* the blue team by three tenths of a second!

**GEORGE.** That's it! From now on, I'm not doing *anything* with Walt around! He ruins *everything!*

**HARRIET.** But he didn't have anything to do with us losing!

**GEORGE.** That doesn't matter. He's just...bad luck!

**HARRIET.** But...

**GEORGE.** Excuse me, but I have a race to go to that I *know* I can win! *(He exits.)*

*(**No. 7A SLED RACE FANFARE** plays.)*

**SUSAN.** And now ladies and gentlemen! It's time for our most exciting race! Downhill sledding! *(She is trying to lighten the mood.)* Now personally, I've never been sure why they call it *downhill* sledding! I've yet to hear of an *uphill* sledding race, but oh well! I'm going to turn it over to Roger who is on top of the hill ready to tell us about our contestants!

*(***SUSAN*** walks over to comfort ***HARRIET***. Everyone goes downstage and sits facing upstage to watch the sledding race. The use of wooden cut out puppets that can be manipulated behind a mountain of snow is effective.)*

**ROGER.** *(V.O.)* Thank you Susan! We have two experienced contestants this year. Our first contestant is the all time record holder, George of the red team. He tells me that he has been training really hard this year.

*(There are some muffled sounds and then we hear* **GEORGE**'s *voice.)*

**GEORGE.** *(V.O.)* That's right, Roger. Practice and sacrifice, sacrifice and practice. And of course lots of carrots. Years and years of...

**ROGER.** *(V.O.)* Yes, uh...thank you George. But you have a race to do right now! On your mark, get set...GO!

*(**No. 7B SLED RACE** Underscore plays.)*

*(The **GEORGE** puppet glides down the hill. All react.)*

He's flying like a bird ladies and gentlemen! Look at him go! Such grace on the slops, such control! There he goes, over the finish line! Wait! Can it be? Why yes, it can! George has broken his own record by four seconds! Unbelievable! Of course, there is another contestant, so anything can happen!

*(During the following, **GEORGE** comes back onstage brushing the snow off of himself. **KIDS** congratulate him. **HARRIET** avoids him. **GEORGE** sits and watches the rest of the race.)*

**ROGER.** *(V.O.)* Ladies and gentlemen! Our second and final contestant is Michelle from the blue team. She has her work cut out for her if she hopes to beat George. She's taken her position and she looks very determined. On your mark, get set, GO!

*(The Michelle puppet goes down the hill. "Hurray! Go Michelle" clapping and cheering, etc. are heard on V.O.)*

What a great start! Michelle has been involved in this race for the past three years. She's continued to improve, but has yet to beat the all time champion, George.

**GEORGE.** Did you hear that everyone? He called me a champion!

**ARNIE.** Wow. You are so lucky.

**GEORGE.** Luck has nothing to do with it. It's practice, Arnie. Practice and sacrifice. Years and years of...

**LOUANNE.** Oh please, George. You're a rabbit. You're supposed to be fast.

(**KIDS** *laugh.*)

**ROGER.** *(V.O.)* Michelle is almost to the finish line! Can she beat George's record? NO! She is behind George by two tenths of a second! What a close race! Once again, the winner of the downhill sledding race is George!

(**KIDS** *stand. Everyone [except* **HARRIET***] congratulates* **GEORGE**. *In the meantime* **WALT** *sneaks offstage.*)

**TINA.** Way to go, George!

**ALL.** *(staggered)* Congratulations! You sure are fast! How do you feel? *(etc.)*

**ROGER.** *(V.O.)* Oh! Excuse me ladies and gentlemen. It seems we have another contestant. I believe he is with the red team, but I'm not sure.

**WALT.** *(V.O.)* Team…beam!

**ROGER.** *(V.O.)* Good rhyming young man! His name is uh…what's your name son?

**WALT.** *(V.O.)* Walt…malt!

**ROGER.** *(V.O.)* All righty, Walt! On your mark, get set, GO!

**HARRIET, NANCY & SUSAN.** *OH NO! IT'S WALT!!!*

(*The* **WALT** *puppet begins skiing down the hill. All watch.*)

**KIDS.** *Walt?!?*

**ROGER.** *(V.O.)* He's off to a great start ladies and gentlemen! He's a little fellow, so he should be able to just fly down the course. Oh my…he seems to be having a little trouble. He appears to be losing control. Oh no. He's swerving…he *is* losing control.

(*Lights shift.* **CROWD** *and puppet freeze during the following:*)

**AUNT SUSAN.** *(V.O.)* Your mom wandered off and ended up on some very thin ice. The second I saw her and yelled her name, the ice cracked and Nancy fell through. We all rushed to her, and I was able to throw her my scarf and pull her out. It was the scariest moment of my life.

*(Lights shift back. **CROWD** moves normally. Puppet bumps a tree and falls over out of sight.)*

**ROGER.** *(V.O.)* It looks like…ohhhh! He's fallen. He's down ladies and gentlemen! Can we please get some assistance?

**NANCY.** WALT!

*(**NANCY** and **SUSAN** run offstage.)*

**ROGER.** *(V.O.)* He's up ladies and gentlemen! He's all right. No need to panic!

**GEORGE.** Ha ha! Of course Walt fell! He doesn't know how to sled! He can only sled with Harriet so he can ruin it for her!

**HARRIET.** *(walks to **GEORGE**)* You know what George? I am sick and tired of your mean comments about my little brother. He could have been hurt! And by the way, I don't want to be your partner at the dance!

*(**HARRIET** runs off. **KIDS** follow leaving **GEORGE** onstage alone.)*

***(No. 7C WHAT WOULD I DO WITHOUT YOU? Scene Shift music plays.)***

## Scene Seven

*(NANCY & SUSAN are decorating for the Winter Carnival Dance. There are snowflake decorations and white lights.)*

NANCY. I'm just so glad that Walt wasn't hurt!

SUSAN. I know. Nobody saw him sneak away.

NANCY. Now that I know he moves faster than a speeding rabbit, I'll just have to keep him on a leash!

SUSAN. It was so nice that Harriet wanted Walt to stay with her today.

NANCY. It *is* nice. She hasn't let him out of her sight!

SUSAN. *(setting up a screen for the slides)* Can you give me a hand with this?

NANCY. Sure. Are the slides ready?

SUSAN. All ready! Do you think the kids will be surprised?

NANCY. They should be. I've kept everything a secret.

SUSAN. Great! I am going to test the music. *(**No. 7D BUST A MOVE Underscore** plays.)* Oh, I love this song! It makes me want to get my groove on!

*(SUSAN begins to dance. NANCY laughs and begins to dance as well. Music gets louder and they go into a full blown choreographed routine. KIDS begin to enter and soon they are all watching. LOUANNE is wearing HARRIET's dress. HARRIET enters with WALT on a leash. HARRIET is embarrassed seeing her Mom dance.)*

HARRIET. *MOM!!! What are you doing?*

NANCY. We were just busting some moves, dear.

HARRIET. Please stop before you bust something else!

*(All laugh.)*

TINA. *(to SUSAN & NANCY)* Wow! You're good dancers!

SUSAN. Thank you, Tina! What excellent taste you have! *(to all)* Welcome to the Winter Carnival Dance! Come in! Have some punch and enjoy!

*(GIRLS walk to one side of the room, BOYS to the other side. SUSAN points to them.)*

Do they still do that?

**NANCY.** What?

**SUSAN.** The boys on one side, the girls on the other.

*(NANCY shrugs.)*

*(NANCY takes WALT off of his leash and gives him some punch.)*

**NANCY.** Have some punch, Walt.

**WALT.** Punch…lunch!

**SUSAN.** Good job, Walt!

**WALT.** Walt…salt!

**NANCY.** Nice!

**WALT.** Nice…mice!

**NANCY.** 'K.

**WALT.** 'K…hay!

**NANCY.** You can stop dear.

**WALT.** Dear…tear!

**SUSAN.** Let's not talk for a while. Maybe he'll slow down.

**NANCY.** Good thinking.

**WALT.** Thinking…stinking!

**HARRIET.** *(to LOUANNE)* So I told George that he was too mean to Walt and that I'm going to the dance alone.

**LOUANNE.** Well, I don't blame you Harriet. That was a scary thing seeing Walt fall.

**HARRIET.** It sure was.

**LOUANNE.** You know what I think? I think that Walt was showing off for you.

**HARRIET.** You do?

**LOUANNE.** Sure! You know how he always wants your attention?

**HARRIET.** Of course.

**LOUANNE.** Well, he sure got it!

**GIRLS.** He sure did!

**ARNIE.** Congratulations on winning the sled race, George.

**GEORGE.** *(sadly)* Thanks.

**OSWALDO.** You sure are fast!

**GEORGE.** Thanks.

**ARNIE.** That was scary about Walt though.

**OSWALDO.** It sure was. He could have really been hurt.

**ARNIE.** He was lucky.

**GEORGE.** Lucky.

**OSWALDO.** Too bad about the Snowman Race.

**GEORGE.** Yeah.

**ARNIE.** You're unusually quiet tonight, George. Everything O.K.?

**GEORGE.** Fine.

**SUSAN.** May I have your attention, please? We have a surprise for you! Come and have a seat.

(**KIDS** *sit facing the upstage screen.*)

**NANCY.** Here we go!

(*Lights dim,* **No. 7E SLIDE SHOW** *Underscore plays, and a large picture of* **TINA** *as a toddler appears on the screen.*)

**ALL.** *(staggered)* Awww! Tina! Look how cute she is! *(etc.)*

**NANCY.** Here's Tina when she was a toddler. Tina, could you please come forward?

(**TINA** *stands beside her picture.*)

Even though her teeth weren't all grown in, Tina was already teething on branches. Tina always has a smile on her face and something nice to say. We have an award to give her for the best smile!

(**NANCY** *gives* **TINA** *an award.* **TINA** *thanks them. All applaud. Picture of* **OSWALDO** *as a baby appears. He is wearing a football helmet and holding a basketball. He looks bewildered.*)

**ALL.** Awww!

**ARNIE.** How come he is wearing a football helmet and holding a basketball?

**OSWALDO.** I'd rather not talk about it.

**SUSAN.** Oswaldo, come on up here!

*(OSWALDO stands beside his picture.)*

SUSAN. As you can see, Oswaldo's love for sports was already apparent at a very young age. We would like to award Oswaldo for being the most willing to try new things!

*(SUSAN gives OSWALDO his award. He thanks them. All applaud. Baby picture of ARNIE appears. He is bundled up so he can barely be seen.)*

LOUANNE. You haven't changed, Arnie!

*(KIDS laugh.)*

OSWALDO. Your turn, Arnie!

*(ARNIE stands beside his picture.)*

NANCY. Here is Arnie bundled up to play outside. Even though we can't always see his face during the winter months, I'm sure that we all agree the award for the warmest dresser goes to him!

*(Award is presented. ARNIE thanks them. All applaud. Baby picture of LOUANNE appears. She is wearing a very colorful dress and looks absolutely thrilled. She rushes over to ARNIE and takes his place.)*

SUSAN. As you can see from this picture of Louanne, she has always had a great outlook on life. She is a wonderful friend to all who know her. This award is for the best attitude!

*(Award is presented. LOUANNE thanks them. All applaud. Baby picture of SYDNEY appears. She is pouring liquid into a test tube and reading a science book.)*

NANCY. Come on up here, Sydney! *(SYDNEY does.)* Sydney began doing science experiments at a very young age. I believe that you accidentally started a few fires, but were able to put them out. Is that right?

SYDNEY. Yes, I was mixing chemicals and being so young, I didn't realize how combustible the combination was. But I always had a fire extinguisher handy. Every home should have one. Or two.

**NANCY.** Yes, well, from those humble beginnings, Sydney has proven to have an amazing capacity for learning and inventing. This award is for the one most likely to succeed!

*(Award is presented.* **SYDNEY** *thanks them. All applaud. Baby picture of* **GEORGE** *appears. He is holding many trophies.)*

**ALL.** Wow!

**ARNIE.** He already had trophies as a baby?

**SUSAN.** Here's the only rabbit that we know who won races before he could hop! George, please stand up.

*(***GEORGE*** sadly crosses to picture.)*

I think that we all know what this trophy is for! George is the fastest sled racer on record! Here's your trophy, George!

*(Award is presented. All applaud.* **GEORGE** *thanks them and quickly walks away. Baby picture of* **HARRIET** *appears. She is wearing a tutu and is doing a dance pose.)*

**ALL.** Awww!

**NANCY.** I am so happy that I get to present this award to my daughter, Harriet. Harriet, please come up.

*(***HARRIET*** does.)*

Being an older sister isn't easy. It takes a lot of tolerance and understanding. As far as I'm concerned, Harriet is the best there is! This award is for being the most patient sister!

*(***NANCY*** gives* **HARRIET** *award. They hug. All applaud. Baby picture of* **WALT** *goes up.)*

**ALL.** Awww!

**SUSAN.** And last but certainly not least, Walt!

*(***WALT*** runs up. All laugh and applaud.)*

**SUSAN.** Walt is just a wonderful bundle of energy. He wants to be older like all of you so much that he can hardly stand to wait! Thank you for being kind to him and showing him friendship. This award is for the one with the best rhymes!

**WALT.** Rhyme...

*(He can't think of a rhyme. He begins to look as if he has a word and everyone reacts. Then he looks frustrated.* **KIDS** *react with disappointment. This happens three times. The third time he thinks of a word.)*

...sublime!

*(All applaud.)*

**ARNIE.** Impressive!

**LOUANNE.** I'll say!

*(***KIDS*** begin talking to each other.* **HARRIET** *walks over to* **SUSAN.***)*

**HARRIET.** Aunt Susan?

**SUSAN.** Yes, dear?

**HARRIET.** I've made a decision. I'm going to give Walt my snow globe when he gets a little older. Just like when you gave your dolly to my mom.

**SUSAN.** Oh Harriet, that is so sweet! The tradition of giving carries on.

*(They hug.)*

**NANCY.** Well, it's the time you've been waiting for! The Winter Carnival Dance! Please find your partner!

**ARNIE.** I'm going to go and ask Louanne to dance. Do you want to come and talk to the girls?

**GEORGE.** No. Walt isn't the only one who learned a lesson today.

**ARNIE.** Uh...O.K. See you, George.

**OSWALDO.** Bye.

*(***ARNIE*** and* **OSWALDO*** cross to* **GIRLS.***)*

*SONG No. 8: WINTER CARNIVAL DANCE (intro)*

*(Large special that looks like a snow globe appears as in opening.)*

(ARNIE & LOUANNE, OSWALDO & SYDNEY *partner up and begin dancing.* HARRIET *stands alone looking around the room. She walks over to* WALT, *takes his hand and leads him to the dance floor.*)

NANCY. Harriet, you are so thoughtful!

SUSAN. Nice, Harriet!

KIDS. Awww!

KIDS. *(sing)*
WE LIKE TO REACH REAL HIGH, THEN TAKE IT DOWN LOW.
DO A JUMP LIKE THIS AND OFF WE GO!
WE STEP TOGETHER STEP AND NEXT WE TURN,
IT'S REALLY FUN TO DO AND NOT HARD TO LEARN!

(TINA *goes to* GEORGE *and guides him to the dance floor.*)

LIFT YOUR SHOULDERS UP, FIRST LEFT THEN RIGHT,
THIS IS SO MUCH FUN THAT WE COULD DANCE ALL NIGHT!
WE STEP, KICK! TURN, HOP AND SKIP,
THEN WE END THIS PART WITH A GRACEFUL DIP.

(GEORGE *walks over to* HARRIET.)

GEORGE. Uh…Harriet? I know, well…I mean…could you, or would you…gosh, this is hard.

HARRIET. George, would you like to dance with me?

GEORGE. Yes!

HARRIET. Tina, would you dance with Walt?

TINA. Happy to! Come on little fellow! Let's dance!

WALT. Dance…pants!

TINA. Good job, Walt!

(TINA *and* WALT *begin dancing.*)

GEORGE. Harriet, I want to apologize for how I treated Walt. I don't blame you for being mad at me.

HARRIET. Thanks, George. I think we've all learned some things this week.

GEORGE. Friends?

*(He extends his right hand.)*

**HARRIET.** Friends.

*(She shakes his hand.)*

**ALL.**
>WE ALL DO A SLIDE THEN CLAP ON THE BEAT.
>TURN TO OUR LEFT, GOTTA MOVE OUR FEET.
>WE TAKE OUR PARTNERS HANDS AND SWING 'EM UP AND DOWN.
>PEOPLE ARE DANCIN' ALL THROUGH THE TOWN!
>
>SHAKE YOUR HANDS LIKE THIS FROM SIDE TO SIDE,
>THE RHYTHM THAT YOU'RE FEELIN' SIMPLY CAN'T BE DENIED!
>WE STEP, KICK! TURN, HOP AND SKIP,
>THEN WE END OUR DANCE WITH A GRACEFUL DIP.
>
>IT'S FINALLY TIME TO DO THE WINTER CARNIVAL DANCE.
>IT'S SO MUCH FUN, YOU'VE GOT TO TAKE A CHANCE.
>TO GET OUT ON THE DANCE FLOOR AND SET YOURSELF FREE.
>DON'T BE SHY (NO, DON'T BE SHY)
>JUST COME (JUST COME) AND DANCE WITH ME!

*(Snow begins falling.* **HARRIET** *notices it.)*

**HARRIET.** Hey, look! *(She points at the snow)* Yippee! It's snowing!

*(**No. 8A YIPPEE! Curtain Call** music plays. Optional: **CAST** sings the last chorus.)*

## The End

## HARRIET AND WALT COSTUME DESIGN

*HARRIET AND WALT*'s costume design focused around creating child friendly animals and Nancy Carlson's original drawings from the book. Having a child's form with animal accents and accessories was the idea for many of the costumes. Animal accessories included: knitted fur ears, fur vests, and painted faces. The design was bright and cheery, and choices were made to reflect the original characters as much as possible.

## SET DESIGN

The original scenic design for *HARRIET AND WALT* was inspired by Nancy Carlson's book illustrations. Referencing her style of color and pattern in the paint treatments, the larger concept was to frame the various scenes within a magical snow globe. The basic locations for the play existed side by side and were controlled with light to focus the action: Harriet's kitchen and living room area, Harriet's bedroom, and Harriet's neighborhood, covered in a blanket of beautiful white snow.

The interior scenes were set far stage right and left and each had a small circular shaped background decorated with wallpaper illustrations from Carlson's books. The exterior snow scene was set center stage inside a large black circular portal. The portal was made of two large half-circle panels that traveled right and left on the traveler track. The circular opening could iris shut so that the snow scene was hidden, or open fully to reveal falling snow, fir and birch trees, and banks of fluffy, glistening snow.

# HARRIET AND WALT SNOWMAN AND SNOWBALL CONSTRUCTION

**The Snowman:**

Due to the need for the snowman to be built and knocked over onstage several times, I decided the best way to build it was in separate pieces. I built three different balls of snow: a round head piece, a larger torso piece with an indentation at the top for the head to rest in and a larger bottom ball with a flat base and another indented top for the torso ball to rest into. Then, as the actors were "making" the snowballs they would roll the head offstage, roll across with the torso, and return with the base thus making it appear that the snowballs were growing in size.

In my construction of the snowman, I chose to make the balls hollow, using a framework of ply wrapped in chicken wire and then covering that with a mache' painted white and then covering that with cotton batting. It would be possible to carve the entire thing out of foam instead, but that is dependent on cost and I was concerned that the foam would break more than the frame would through repeated abuse.

The only other helpful elements I added to this were the use of some decent magnets and metal plating. I added magnets to the indented sections and metal plating to the base of the torso and head to stabilize the entire snowman, so that it would only fall apart when it needed to. I also put metal plating on the places where the coal was supposed to go. The coal pieces were carved and painted foam with magnets on the back to stick to the plating.

For the stick arms and the carrot I had pipe running through the snowman for these pieces to sleeve through.

**The Snowballs:**

I tried a couple of options for the thrown snow balls, but the version we sided with was carved foam rubber balls painted white and then hidden in bins onstage. The bins also had some of that "magic snow" product that looks like snow when water is added. This created a nice spray when thrown or when it hit an actor. This created a nice effect without getting the stage too slick and dangerous for the actors (as real snow has a tendency of doing).